DIABETIC COOKBOOK
FOR BEGINNERS

Live a happy and Care-Free Life from Diabetes with this Book of DIABETIC COOKBOOK for BEGINNERS which Includes 40+ Mouth-Watering, Quick, and Easy recipes for beginners of Any Age.

Table of content

INTRODUCTION

Meals are something regular and in the event that you can exploit it to improve your wellbeing and shed pounds, it is the greater part the fight won against diabetes. The Diabetic Cookbook for Beginners is the ideal manual for begin!

With an ever increasing number of adolescents determined to have diabetes, there is an unexpected need to figure out how to control and forestall the infection before its beginning. The thought behind this cookbook is to control the infections at its early stage. While those numbers are disturbing, fortunately you can cook and eat your approach to better wellbeing and this book makes it simple. Make in excess of 100 delectable plans, large numbers of which cook shortly or less.

Diabetic Meal Prep for Beginners gives the best, most delicious, and fastest supper alternatives to control and vanquish your diabetes. The plans included here in this diabetic cookbook take a gander at that greater picture. Regardless of whether utilizing this diabetic cookbook for breakfast or the snacks in the middle of dinners, you will discover heavenly alternatives that work with your timetable.

This cookbook presents a simple to-follow diet intend to keep away from results and keep up typical glucose levels. You will be amazed by the measure of sound yet flavourful plans you can get ready rapidly and effectively at home.

It's especially conceivable to plan sound and eat delectable dinners that keep blood glucose levels in a safe range. This diabetic cookbook extraordinarily composed by a clinical specialist is explicitly intended for all diabetic patients who need to assume responsibility for their glucose levels and start-up another diabetic-accommodating dietary patterns. With a major guarantee that none of these brilliant plans will take you over 30 minutes to cook, this cookbook is likewise an extraordinary asset for occupied people. This incredible cookbook offers plans and supper designs as well as direction and tips to proactively handle this sickness.

This cookbook will assist you with: How To Manage Diabetes If You Have Just Been Diagnosed A Healthy Meal Can Help Reduce the Effects of Diabetes The Basics of Meal Prep Breakfast Recipes Lunch Recipes Dinner Recipes Salad Recipes Appetizers and snacks. All the suppers in this guide have been contemplated and tried to forestall and control diabetes, stay solid and lift energy, and afterward live better. The Diabetes Cookbook For beginners provides all of the details you'll need to prepare healthy, diabetic-friendly meals.

RECIPES

1. Healthy Green Smoothie with Chia and Peach | Dairy-Free, No Added Sugar

Prep Time: 5 mins / Cook Time 5 mins/ Servings: 1

Ingredients
- 1 tbsp. chia seeds
- 1 banana ripe, ideally frozen
- 1 peach chopped, ripe
- 1 cup unsweetened almond milk cold
- 1 cup spinach fresh, washed

Directions

1. In a blender, combine all of the ingredients in the order mentioned, with the greens on the bottom near the blade to help them blend smoother, and the chia seeds on the bottom to absorb some liquid before blending.

2. Allow for a few minutes for the chia seeds to absorb the almond milk.

3. Combine all ingredients in a blender and serve with your favourite toppings. Take pleasure in it.

Nutritional Values:

Calories 241
Calories from Fat 63 %
Fat 7g
Saturated Fat 0.2g
Polyunsaturated Fat 0.2g
Monounsaturated Fat 0.1g
Sodium 195mg
Potassium 779mg
Carbohydrates 43g
Fibre 10g
Sugar 23g
Protein 6g
Vitamin A 3200IU
Vitamin C 34.7mg
Calcium 690mg
Iron 1.4mg

2. **Crunchy Oven-Baked Tilapia**

Prep Time: 15 mins / Cook Time 10 mins/ Servings: 4

Ingredients
- 4 tilapia fillets (6 ounces each)
- 1 tablespoon reduced-fat mayonnaise
- 1 tablespoon lime juice
- 1/4 teaspoon grated lime zest
- 1/2 teaspoon salt
- 1/4 teaspoon onion powder
- 1/4 teaspoon pepper
- 1/2 cup panko bread crumbs
- Cooking spray
- 2 tablespoons minced fresh cilantro or parsley

Directions

1. Preheat the oven to 425 degrees Fahrenheit. Place the fillets on a baking sheet that has been sprayed with non-stick cooking spray.

2. Combine the mayonnaise, lime juice and zest, salt, onion powder, and pepper in a small cup. Apply the mayonnaise mixture to the fish. Spritz with cooking spray and cover with bread crumbs.

3. Bake for 15-20 minutes, or until the fish starts to flake easily with a fork. Garnish with chopped cilantro.

Nutritional Values

1 fillet: 186 calories
3g fat
1g saturated fat
84mg cholesterol
401mg sodium
6g carbohydrate
0 sugars
0 fibre
33g protein.

3. **Healthy Granola**

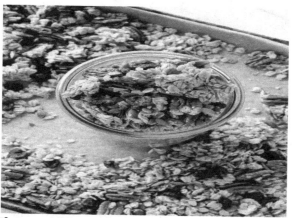

Prep Time: 10 mins / Cook Time 16 mins/ Servings: 8 cups (16)

Ingredients

- 4 cups old-fashioned rolled oats (use certified gluten-free oats for gluten-free granola)
- 1 ½ cup raw nuts and/or seeds
- 1 teaspoon fine-grain sea salt (if you're using standard table salt, scale back to ¾ teaspoon)
- ½ teaspoon ground cinnamon
- ½ cup melted coconut oil or olive oil
- ½ cup maple syrup or honey
- 1 teaspoon vanilla extract
- ⅔ Cup dried fruit, chopped if large (like dried cranberries)
- Totally optional additional mix-ins: ½ cup chocolate chips or coconut flakes*

Directions

1. Preheat the oven to 350°F and line a wide rimmed baking sheet with parchment paper.

2. Combine the oats, nuts and/or seeds, salt, and cinnamon in a big mixing bowl. To combine the ingredients, stir them together.

3. Combine the oil, maple syrup and/or honey, and vanilla extract in a mixing bowl. Mix until all of the oats and nuts are finely covered. Pour the granola into the prepared pan and spread it out evenly with a wide spoon.

4. Bake for 21 to 24 minutes, stirring halfway through (for extra-clumpy granola, press the stirred granola down with your spatula to create a more even layer). When the granola cools, it will become even crispier.

5. Allow the granola to cool fully without being disturbed (at least 45 minutes). Place the dried fruit on top (and optional chocolate chips, if using).

6. If you want large chunks of granola, break it up with your hands; if you don't want granola that's too clumpy, stir it with a spoon.

7. For 1 to 2 weeks at room temperature, or up to 3 months in the freezer, store the granola in an airtight jar. Allow for 5 to 10 minutes for the dried fruit to come to room temperature before serving.

Nutritional Values

Calories 234
Saturated Fat 6.3g
Polyunsaturated Fat 1.6g
Monounsaturated Fat 3.1g
Cholesterol 0mg
Sodium 134.4mg
Total Carbohydrate 27.6g
Dietary Fibre 3.4g
Protein 3.5g

4. Tortilla Pie

Prep Time: 15 mins / Cook Time 15 mins/ Servings: 4

Ingredients

- 1/2 pound lean ground beef (90% lean)
- 1/2 cup chopped onion
- 2 garlic cloves, minced
- 1 teaspoon chili powder
- 1/2 teaspoon ground cumin
- 1 can (14-1/2 ounces) Mexican diced tomatoes, drained
- 3/4 cup reduced-fat ricotta cheese
- 1/4 cup shredded part-skim mozzarella cheese
- 3 tablespoons minced fresh cilantro, divided
- 4 whole wheat tortillas (8 inches)
- 1/2 cup shredded cheddar cheese

Directions

1. Preheat the oven to 400 degrees Fahrenheit (200 degrees Celsius). Cook the beef, onion, and garlic in a large skillet over medium heat until the beef is no longer pink, about 4-6 minutes.

2. Toss in the tomatoes and seasonings. Bring the water to a boil, then turn off the heat. Combine ricotta, mozzarella, and 2 tablespoons cilantro in a small mixing bowl.1 tortilla, sprayed with cooking spray, in a 9-inch round baking pan.

3. Half of the meat sauce, 1 tortilla, ricotta mixture, another tortilla, and the rest of the meat sauce are layered on top.

4. Top with the remaining tortilla and the remaining cilantro and cheddar cheese.

5. Cover and bake for 15-20 minutes, or until completely heated.

Nutritional Values

1 serving: 356 calories
 14g fat
6g saturated fat
65mg cholesterol
574mg sodium
32g carbohydrate
7g sugars
5g fibre
25g protein.

5. **Basic Vinaigrette**

Prep Time: 5 mins / Cook Time 5 mins/ Servings: 1/2 cups

Ingredients
- 1 tsp. garlic, minced (1-2 cloves)
- 1 tsp. Dijon Mustard
- 2 TBP Champagne vinegar
- 6 TBP Extra Virgin Olive Oil
- Sea Salt, freshly ground
- Black pepper, freshly ground

Directions

1. If you're going to use the dressing right away, combine all of the ingredients in a cup, except the olive oil.

2. Then, in a steady wind, drizzle in the EVOO. Otherwise, combine all of the ingredients in a jar with a tight-fitting lid and shake to emulsify the oil.

3. It's about the taste. Season with salt and pepper.

NUTRITIONAL-VALUE

Calories 184
Fat 21g
Carb 1g

6. **Easy Pea & Spinach Carbonara**

Prep Time: 10 mins / Cook Time 10 mins/
Servings: 4

Ingredients

- 1 ½ tablespoons extra-virgin olive oil
- ½ cup panko breadcrumbs, preferably whole-wheat
- 1 small clove garlic, minced
- 8 tablespoons grated Parmesan cheese, divided
- 3 tablespoons finely chopped fresh parsley
- 3 large egg yolks
- 1 large egg
- ½ teaspoon ground pepper
- ¼ teaspoon salt
- 1 (9 ounce) package fresh tagliatelle or linguine
- 8 cups baby spinach
- 1 cup peas (fresh or frozen)

Directions

1. In a big pot, put 10 cups of water to a high boil.

2. In a big skillet, heat the oil over medium-high heat in the meantime. Cook, stirring constantly, for 2 minutes, or until breadcrumbs and garlic are toasted.

3. 2 teaspoons Parmesan and parsley should be added to a small bowl. Delete the item from circulation.

4. In a medium mixing bowl, combine the remaining 6 tablespoons Parmesan, the milk yolks, the egg, the pepper, and salt. In a pot of boiling water, cook the pasta for 1 minute, stirring occasionally.

5. Cook for 1 minute more after adding the spinach and peas, until the pasta is soft. 1/4 cup boiling water should be set aside. Place in a large mixing bowl after draining.

6. Whisk the egg mixture slowly with the reserved cooking water. Toss the pasta with tongs as you gradually apply the mixture to it. Top with the breadcrumb mixture that was set aside.

Nutritional Values
430 calories
Protein 20.2g
Carbohydrates 54.1g
Dietary fibre 8.2g
Sugars 2.5g
Fat 14.5g
Saturated fat 3.9g
Cholesterol 223.4mg
Vitamin a in 8198IU
Vitamin c 50.5mg
Folate 53mcg
Calcium 246.1mg
Iron 6.1mg
Magnesium 99.6mg
Potassium 160mg
Sodium 586.4mg.

7. **Roasted Brussels sprouts with Goat Cheese & Pomegranate**

Prep Time: 15 mins / Cook Time 20 mins/ Servings: 4

Ingredients

- 1 pound Brussels sprouts, trimmed and halved
- 1 large shallot, sliced
- 1 tablespoon extra-virgin olive oil
- ¼ teaspoon salt
- ¼ teaspoon ground pepper
- 2-3 teaspoons white balsamic vinegar
- ⅓ cup crumbled goat cheese
- ¼ cup pomegranate seeds

Directions

1. Preheat the oven to 400 degrees Fahrenheit (200 degrees Celsius).

2. In a medium mixing bowl, combine the Brussels sprouts, shallot, oil, salt, and pepper. Using a broad rimmed baking sheet, spread the mixture out evenly.

3. 20 to 22 minutes to roast the Brussels sprouts until tender.

4. Toss with vinegar to taste in the mixing bowl. Add pomegranate seeds and goat cheese to finish.

Nutritional-Value

117 calories
Protein 5.8g
Carbohydrates 13.6g
Dietary fibre 4.8g
Sugars 4.5g
Fat 5.7g
Saturated fat 1.8g
Cholesterol 4.1mg
Vitamin a in 1006.8IU
Vitamin c 97.9mg
Folate 76.1mcg
Calcium 64.4mg
Iron 1.9mg
Magnesium 30.4mg
Potassium 490.8mg
Sodium 216mg
Thiamine 0.2mg.

8. **Easy Garlic Basil Shrimp**

Prep Time 20 minutes/ Cook Time 7 minutes/ Servings 4

Ingredients
- 1 pound shrimp deveined,   peeled,   and defrosted
- 2 tablespoons butter quantity divided
- Sea salt
- Freshly ground pepper
- 1 clove garlic crushed
- 2 tablespoons lemon juice
- 2 tablespoons basil minced
- 1/8 teaspoon chili pepper flakes
- 1 teaspoon lemon zest

Directions

1. Towel-dry the shrimp. Over medium-high heat, heat a large skillet. 1 tablespoon margarine (reserving the other tablespoon for later).

2. Add shrimp to the pan until the butter has melted and stopped foaming. Make sure the pan isn't overcrowding.

3. It's not a good idea for shrimp to come into contact with one another. Cook the shrimp in small batches if possible.

4. Add a pinch of salt and pepper to the shrimp. Allow 2-3 minutes for the first side of the shrimp to brown without moving, then flip.

5. Remove the shrimp to a plate and set aside until they are completely cooked (about 2-3 minutes longer).

6. Lower the sun. In a separate pan, melt the remaining tablespoon of butter.

7. Add garlic until the butter has ceased to foam. Cook for approximately 1 minute.

8. Cook, scraping up browned bits as needed, until liquid has almost completely evaporated. In a large mixing bowl, combine the shrimp and any liquids that have collected on the pan.

9. Remove the skillet from the heat and add the basil, chili flakes, and lemon zest. To taste, season with salt and pepper.

Per serving:
Calories: 134
Fat (g): 7
Carbs (g): 2
Fibre (g): 0
Protein (g): 15
Net carbs (g):2

9. **Baked Garlic Scampi**

Preparation time: About 5 minutes/ Cook time: 10 minutes/ Servings: 4

Ingredients

- 1 tablespoon extra-virgin olive oil
- 1/4 teaspoon salt
- 7 garlic cloves, crushed
- 2 tablespoons chopped fresh parsley, divided
- 1 pound large shrimp, shelled (with tails left on) and deveined
- Juice and zest of 1 lemon
- 2 cups baby arugula

Directions

1. Preheat oven to 350 degrees Fahrenheit. Using the olive oil, grease a 13-x-9-x-2-inch baking tray.

2. In a medium mixing bowl, combine the salt, garlic, and 1 tablespoon parsley; stir well and set aside.

3. In a baking pan, arrange the shrimp in a single layer and bake for 3 minutes, uncovered.

4. Turn the shrimp over and top with the remaining 1 tablespoon of parsley, lemon peel, and lemon juice.

5. Bake for an additional 1–2 minutes, or until the shrimp are bright pink and tender.

6. Take the shrimp out of the oven. Serve the arugula with the shrimp on a serving platter. Serve the shrimp and arugula with the garlic mixture on top.

Nutritional Values:

Calories 110
Fat 3.5g
Saturated Fat 0.5g
Trans Fat 0.0g
Cholesterol 120mg
Sodium 220mg
Potassium 250mg
Total Carbohydrate 3g
Dietary Fibre 0g
Sugars 1g
Protein 16g
Phosphorus 165mg.

10.   **Baked Rotisserie Chicken**

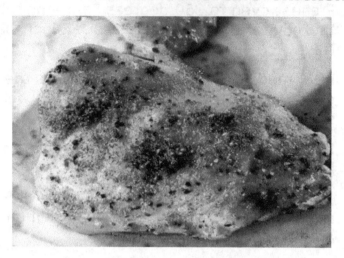

Prep Time: 10 minutes Cook Time: 45 minutes Total Time: 55 minutes Servings: 8

Ingredients

- 3-4 pound chicken gizzards removed
- 2 tablespoons canola oil or melted butter
- For the Dry Rub
- 2 teaspoons pepper
- 1 tablespoon garlic powder
- 1 tablespoon kosher salt
- 1 tablespoon onion powder
- 1 tablespoon paprika
- Dash of cayenne pepper
- 1 teaspoon dried thyme

Directions

1. Preheat the oven to 375 degrees Fahrenheit.

2. Place the chicken in a metal baking pan lined with foil or parchment paper (you can also use a disposable foil pan if desired).

3. Rotisserie seasoning should be applied to both sides of the chicken bits.

4. Roast for 45-60 minutes, or until chicken is completely cooked and thermometer reads 165 degrees F.

Nutritional Values:

Calories: 310kcal
Carbohydrates: 1g
Protein: 27g
Fat: 21g
Saturated Fat: 6g
Cholesterol: 106mg
Sodium: 100mg
Potassium: 291mg
Fibre: 1g
Sugar: 1g
Vitamin A: 230IU
Vitamin C: 2mg
Calcium: 45mg
Iron: 2mg

11.   Lemon Chicken Piccata

Prep Time: 10 minutes Cook Time: 20 minutes
Total Time: 30 minutes Servings: 4

Ingredients
- 2 skinless, boneless chicken breasts
- 3 tbsp. unsalted butter
- 1½ tbsp. all-purpose flour
- ¼ tsp. white pepper
- ¼ tsp. salt
- 2 tbsp. olive oil
- ⅓ Cup dry white wine
- ⅓ Cup low sodium chicken stock
- ¼ cup lemon juice
- ¼ cup drained capers
- ¼ cup Italian Parsley (minced)
- Salt & pepper

Directions

1. Every chicken breast should be sliced in half lengthwise to yield two thin slices.

2. Flatten the chicken breasts with a mallet or other heavy object if possible, to around 12 inch (1.25 cm) thickness.

3. Using a small amount of flour seasoned with salt and pepper, dredge the chicken breast slices. A light dusting is all that is needed, not a heavy coat. Add oil to a large sauté pan that has been heated to medium-high heat.

4. Add the chicken breast slices to the pan until the oil is shimmering. Cook for 3-4 minutes per hand, or until browned and thoroughly cooked. Put the chicken slices aside after removing them from the pan.

5. Over medium-high heat, warm a broad sauté pan. Add the chicken breast slices to the pan until the oil is shimmering.

6. Cook for 3–4 minutes, or until golden brown. Brown the other side of the chicken slices as well. Put the chicken slices aside after removing them from the pan.

7. Stir in the wine in the sauté pan, picking up any browned bits from the rim.

8. Lemon juice and chicken stock should be added at this stage. Raise the heat to maximum and cook for 3 minutes, or until the sauce thickens.

9. Reduce the heat to low and stir in the butter. Return the chicken to the pan to reheat after stirring in the capers and parsley. Season to taste with salt and pepper.

Nutritional Values:

Amount per Serving Calories 269
Fat 15.6g
Saturated Fat 6.6g
Trans Fat 0g
Polyunsaturated Fat 1.5g
Monounsaturated Fat 7.2g
Cholesterol 72.6mg
Sodium 459.5mg
Potassium 259.7mg
Carbohydrates 3.4g
Fibre 0.6g
Sugar 0.4g
Protein 20.3g
Vitamin A 460IU
Vitamin C 8.3mg
Calcium 16mg
Iron 0.9mg
Net carbs 2.8g

12.   Chili Steak & Peppers

Prep Time: 15 minutes Cook Time: 15 minutes Total Time: 30 minutes Servings: 4

Ingredients

- 2 tablespoons chili sauce
- 1 tablespoon lime juice
- 1 teaspoon brown sugar
- 1/2 teaspoon crushed red pepper flakes
- 1/2 teaspoon salt, divided
- 1 beef top sirloin steak (1-1/4 pounds)
- 1 medium onion, halved and sliced
- 1 medium green pepper, cut into strips
- 1 medium sweet yellow pepper, cut into strips
- 2 teaspoons olive oil
- 1 small garlic clove, minced
- 1/8 teaspoon pepper
- 1/4 cup reduced-fat sour cream
- 1 teaspoon prepared horseradish

Directions

1. Brush the steak with a mixture of chili sauce, lime juice, brown sugar, pepper flakes, and 1/4 teaspoon salt. Sautee steaks 4-6 inches from the heat for 5-7 minutes per side or till desired doneness is achieved.

2. A thermometer should read 135° for medium-rare, 140° for medium, and 145° for medium-well.

3. In the meantime, cook onion, green and yellow peppers, and garlic in oil in a large skillet until tender. Cook for 1 minute longer with the garlic, pepper, and the remaining salt.

4. Toss the sour cream and horseradish together in a small mixing bowl. Slice the steak and serve it with the pepper sauce and the pepper mixture.

Nutritional Values:

265 calories
9g fat
3g saturated fat
62mg cholesterol
491mg sodium
12g carbohydrate
8g sugars
2g fibre
32g protein
Diabetic Exchanges: 4 lean meat, 1 vegetable, 1 fat.

13. Sheet-Pan Chili-Lime Salmon with Potatoes & Peppers

Prep Time: 10 minutes Cook Time: 15 minutes
Total Time: 25 minutes Servings: 4

Ingredients

- 1 pound Yukon Gold potatoes, cut into 3/4-inch pieces
- 2 tablespoons extra-virgin olive oil, divided
- ¾ teaspoon salt, divided
- ¼ teaspoon ground pepper
- 2 teaspoons chili powder
- 1 teaspoon ground cumin
- ½ teaspoon garlic powder
- 1 lime, zested and quartered
- 2 medium bell peppers, any colour, sliced
- 1 ¼ pounds centre-cut salmon fillet, skinned, if desired, and cut into 4 portion

Directions

1. Preheat the oven to 425 degrees Fahrenheit (200 degrees Celsius).

2. Using cooking spray, spray a wide rimmed baking sheet.

3. In a medium mixing bowl, combine the potatoes, 1 tablespoon oil, and 1/4 teaspoon salt and pepper. Roast for 15 minutes after transferring to the prepared plate.

4. In a small cup, add the remaining 1/2 teaspoon salt, chilli powder, cumin, garlic powder, lime zest, and chilli powder.

5. Toss the bell peppers with the remaining 1 tablespoon oil and 1/2 tablespoon spice mixture in a medium mixing bowl until well coated. Use the remaining spice mixture to coat the salmon.

6. Removing the pan from the oven after 15 minutes. Stir in the peppers. 5 minutes at 350°F Remove the pan from the oven, and add the salmon along with some of the vegetables.

7. Roast for 6 to 8 minutes, or until the salmon is just cooked through. Serve with lime wedges on the side.

Nutritional-Value

405 calories
Protein 35.4g
Carbohydrates 25.9g
Dietary fibre 3g
Sugars 3.5g
Fat 17.4g
Saturated fat 2.6g
Cholesterol 89.6mg
Vitamin a in 2034.6IU
Vitamin c 85.9mg
Folate 81.4mcg
Calcium 45.7mg
Iron 3mg
Magnesium 83.6mg
Potassium 1426.8mg
Sodium 516.6mg.

14.   Lamb Chops with Orange Sauce

Preparation   time: About   5   minutes   plus marinating   time/   Cook   time: 20   minutes Servings: 4

Ingredients

- 1/2 cup freshly squeezed orange juice
- 2 tablespoons orange zest
- 1 teaspoon fresh or 1/2 teaspoon dried thyme
- 1/8 teaspoon freshly ground black pepper
- Non-stick cooking spray
- 8 small lean lamb chops, about 1/2-inch thick (about 4 ounces each)
- 1 cup sliced fresh mushrooms
- 1/2 cup dry white wine

Directions

1. Combine the orange juice, orange zest, thyme, and pepper in a shallow baking dish and stir well.

2. Trim the lamb chops of any excess fat and put them in a baking dish. Cover the chops with the orange juice mixture and refrigerate for 3–4 hours, turning them periodically.

3. Using non-stick cooking spray, coat a large skillet and fire over medium-high heat until light.

4. Take out the chops from the marinade and set them in the skillet, reserving the marinade. Remove the chops from the skillet and place them on a plate lined with paper towels after browning them on both sides.

5. Reduce the heat to medium-low and add the mushrooms, cooking until they are only tender. Bring to a boil, stirring in the reserved marinade and wine.

6. Come back the lamb chops to the skillet, cover, and cook for 10–12 minutes, or until the sauce has been reduced to about 1/2 cup. Serve the lamb chops on a platter with the orange sauce spooned on top.

Nutritional Values
1/2 Carbohydrate
4 Lean Protein
1/2 Fat
Calories 250 (from Fat 90)
Fat 10g
Saturated 3.5g
Trans 0.0g
Cholesterol 95mg
Sodium 85mg
Potassium 510mg
Total Carbohydrate 5g
Dietary Fibre 1g
Sugars 3g

15. **Veggie & Hummus Sandwich**

Preparation time: 10 minutes/ Cook time: 10 minutes/ Servings: 1

Ingredients
- 2 slices whole-grain bread
- 3 tablespoons hummus
- ¼ avocado, mashed
- ½ cup mixed salad greens
- ¼ medium red bell pepper, sliced
- ¼ cup sliced cucumber
- ¼ cup shredded carrot

Directions
1. Spread hummus on one slice and avocado on the other.

2. Greens, bell pepper, cucumber, and carrot can all be used to make the sandwich.

3. Serve by cutting in half.

Nutritional-Values:

325 calories
Protein 12.8g
Carbohydrates 39.7g
Dietary fibre 12.1g
Sugars 6.8g
Fat 14.3g
Saturated fat 2.2g
Vitamin a in 6388.1IU
Vitamin c 49.8mg
Folate 171.1mcg
Calcium 107.8mg
Iron 3.4mg
Magnesium 105.3mg
Potassium 746.3mg
Sodium 407mg
Thiamine 0.3mg

16. Mediterranean Breakfast Sandwiches

Preparation time: 5 minutes/ Cook time: 15 minutes/ Servings: 4

Ingredients

- 4 multigrain sandwich thins
- 4 teaspoons olive oil
- 1 tablespoon snipped fresh rosemary or 1/2 teaspoon dried rosemary, crushe
- 4 egg
- 2 cups fresh baby spinach leave
- 1 medium tomato, cut into 8 thin slice
- 4 tablespoons reduced-fat feta cheese
- ⅛ teaspoon kosher salt
- Freshly ground black pepper

Directions

1. Preheat the oven to 375 degrees Fahrenheit. Brush the cut sides of the sandwich thins with 2 teaspoons of olive oil.

2. Place on a baking sheet and toast for 5 minutes, or until light brown and crisp around the edges.

3. Meanwhile, heat the remaining 2 teaspoons olive oil and rosemary in a large skillet over medium-high heat. One by one, crack eggs into the skillet.

4. Cook for 1 minute, or until the whites are firm but the yolks are still runny. Using a spatula, break yolks. Cook until the eggs are set on the other side. Switch off the burner.

5. On four serving plates, arrange the bottom halves of toasted sandwich thins. On bowls, divide the spinach between the sandwiches thins.

6. Two tomato slices, an egg, and 1 tablespoon feta cheese are placed on top of each.

7. Add salt and pepper to taste. Sandwich thin halves from the remaining sandwich halves should be layered on top.

Nutritional Values

Per Serving:
242 Calories;
Protein 13g;
Carbohydrates 25g;
Dietary Fiber 6.2g;
Sugars 3.2g;
Fat 11.7g; Saturated Fat 2.9g;
Cholesterol 214mg;
Vitamin A in 2448.4 IU;
Vitamin C 12mg; Folate 28.7mcg;
Calcium 123.2mg;
Iron 3mg; Magnesium 9.9mg;
Potassium 143.8mg;
Sodium 501.2mg

17.   Asian Lettuce Wraps

__Preparation time: 10 minutes/ Cook time: 15 minutes/ Servings: 4__

Ingredients
- 1 tablespoon canola oil
- 1 pound lean ground turkey
- 1 jalapeno pepper, seeded and minced
- 2 green onions, thinly sliced
- 2 garlic cloves, minced
- 2 tablespoons minced fresh basil
- 2 tablespoons lime juice
- 2 tablespoons reduced-sodium soy sauce
- 1 to 2 tablespoons chili garlic sauce
- 1 tablespoon sugar or sugar substitute blend equivalent to 1 tablespoon sugar
- 12 Bib or Boston lettuce leaves
- 1 medium cucumber, julienned
- 1 medium carrot, julienned
- 2 cups bean sprouts

Directions

1. Heat the oil in a large skillet over medium heat. Cook for 6-8 minutes, or until turkey is no longer pink and crumbles easily.

2. Cook for another 2 minutes after adding the jalapeno, green onions, and garlic. Heat through basil, lime juice, soy sauce, chili garlic sauce, and sugar.

3. To serve, stuff lettuce leaves with turkey mixture and cucumber, carrot, and bean sprouts. Fold the lettuce over the filling and tuck it in.

Nutritional Value:

3 lettuce wraps: 259 calories, 12g fat (3g saturated fat), 78mg cholesterol, 503mg sodium, 12g carbohydrate (6g sugars, 3g fibre), and 26g protein. Diabetic Exchanges: 3 lean meat, 1 vegetable, 1/2 starch, 1/2 fat.

18. Charred Shrimp & Pesto Buddha Bowls

Preparation time: 15 minutes/ Cook time: 10 minutes/ Servings: 4

Ingredients
- ⅓ cup prepared pesto
- 2 tablespoons balsamic vinegar
- 1 tablespoon extra-virgin olive oil
- ½ teaspoon salt
- ¼ teaspoon ground pepper
- 1 pound peeled and deveined large shrimp (16-20 count), patted dry
- 4 cups arugula
- 2 cups cooked quinoa
- 1 cup halved cherry tomatoes
- 1 avocado, diced

Directions

1. In a big mixing bowl, combine the pesto, vinegar, oil, salt, and pepper. 4 tablespoons of the mixture should be transferred to a small bowl; set both bowls aside.

2. Over medium-high heat, heat a large cast-iron skillet. Add the shrimp and cook, stirring occasionally, for 4 to 5 minutes, or until just cooked through with a faint char. Place on a tray.

3. Toss the arugula and quinoa with the vinaigrette in a big mixing bowl to cover.

4. Separate the arugula mixture into four cups. Tomatoes, avocado, and shrimp go on top. 1 tablespoon of the reserved pesto mixture should be drizzled over each dish.

Nutritional Value:
Serving Size: 2 1/2 Cups

Per Serving: 429 calories; protein 30.9g; carbohydrates 29.3g; dietary fibre 7.2g; sugars 5g; fat 22g; saturated fat 3.6g; cholesterol 187.5mg; vitamin a in 1125.6IU; vitamin c 14.4mg; folate 108.9mcg; calcium 205.4mg; iron 2.9mg; magnesium 130.5mg; potassium 901.1mg; sodium 571.4mg; thiamine 0.2mg.

19.   Chicken & chorizo jambalaya

Preparation and cooking time Prep: 10 mins Cook: 45 mins Easy Serves 4

Ingredients
- 1 tbsp. olive oil
- 2 chicken breasts, chopped
- 1 onion, diced
- 1 red pepper, thinly sliced
- 2 garlic cloves, crushed
- 75g chorizo, sliced
- 1 tbsp. Cajun seasoning
- 250g long grain rice
- 400g can plum tomato
- 350ml chicken stock

Directions

1. 2 chopped chicken breasts, browned in 1 tbsp. olive oil in a big frying pan with a lid for 5-8 minutes until golden.

2. Remove the item and place it on the counter. Cook for 3-4 minutes, until the onion has softened.

3. Cook for an additional 5 minutes after adding 1 thinly sliced red pepper, 2 crushed garlic cloves, 75g sliced chorizo, and 1 tablespoon Cajun seasoning.

4. Combine the 250g long grain rice, 400g canned tomatoes, and 350ml chicken stock in a mixing bowl. Simmer, covered, for 20-25 minutes, or until rice is tender.

Nutritional Values:
 Per serving:
Kcal 445
Fat 10g
Saturates 3g
Carbs 64g
Sugars 7g
Fibre 2g
Protein 30g
Low in salt 1.2g

20. Low-Carb General Tso's Chicken

Prep Time: 5 minutes Cook Time: 5 minutes Total Time: 10 minutes Servings: 5

Ingredients
SAUCE:
- 2 tablespoons low-sodium tamari or soy sauce
- 1 tablespoon hoisin sauce
- 1 tablespoon ketchup
- 1 tablespoon Thai chili sauce
- 1 teaspoon light brown sugar

CHICKEN:
- 2 skinless boneless chicken breasts, cut into ½-inch cubes
- Kosher salt
- Ground white pepper
- 1 tablespoon corn-starch
- 1 tablespoon peanut oil
- 1 clove garlic (minced)
- 4 dried red chilies
- 1 tablespoon dry sherry
- 4 scallions (chopped)

Directions

1. Mix the sauce ingredients together in a small bowl. Set aside after mixing thoroughly.

2. Season the chicken cubes with salt and white pepper in a medium mixing dish. Set aside after adding the corn starch and thoroughly mixing it in.

3. Over high heat, heat a wok or big skillet. Add the peanut oil once it has reached a high temperature.

4. Stir in the garlic and red chillies for a few seconds, then add the chicken and cook for a few minutes, stirring occasionally.

5. Bring the mixture to a boil with the sauce.

6. Reduce the heat to low and continue to cook for another minute or two, or until the chicken is cooked through and the sauce has thickened.

7. To serve, remove the pan from the oven, toss in the scallions, and discard the red chillies.

Nutritional Values:

(1 serving) Calories 313
Calories from Fat 74 %
Fat 8.2g
Saturated Fat 1.2g
Trans Fat 0g
Polyunsaturated Fat 2.2g
Monounsaturated Fat 3.1g
Cholesterol 86.7mg
Sodium 990.2mg
Potassium 463.8mg
Carbohydrates 18.3g
Fibre 1g
Sugar 10.4g

Protein 33.6g
Vitamin A 0IU
Vitamin C 0mg
Calcium 0mg
Iron 0mg
Net carbs 17.3g

21. Chicken Veggie Stir Fry + the Pre-Diabetes Diet Plan

Prep Time: 15 minutes Cook Time: 15 minutes Total Time: 30 minutes Servings: 6

Ingredients

- 2 tablespoons reduced-sodium soy sauce, divided
- 1 tablespoon minced fresh ginger
- Juice of 1 lime, divided
- 2 teaspoons sesame oil, divided
- 1 pound skinless, boneless chicken breast, cut into bite-size pieces
- 1 tablespoon expeller pressed canola oil
- 2 carrots, cut into very thin rounds (about 1 cup)
- 2 cups bite-size broccoli florets (from 1 small bunch)
- 1 medium zucchini, cut in half lengthwise and then cut into ¼-inch-thick half-moons (about 2 cups)

- 4 garlic cloves, minced
- 2 green onions cut into ¼-inch pieces (white and green parts)
- 1 jalapeño pepper, seeded and minced
- ¼ cup sliced fresh basil
- ¼ cup chopped fresh cilantro
- Brown rice, optional

Directions:

1. In a big zip-top plastic bag or cup, combine 1 tablespoon soy sauce, ginger, half a lime's juice, and 1 teaspoon sesame oil. Refrigerate for 1 hour or up to 24 hours after adding the chicken pieces to the container.

2. Heat the oil in a large wok or non-stick skillet over medium-high heat when you're ready to make your stir fry. Stir in the chicken and the marinade for one minute.

3. Stir in the carrots, broccoli, zucchini, garlic, green onions, and jalapeno pepper for an additional 7 minutes, or until the chicken is cooked through and the vegetables are crisp tender.

4. 1 tablespoon soy sauce, the remaining lime juice, and the remaining sesame oil add the basil and cilantro right before serving.

5. If needed, serve over brown rice.

Nutritional Value:

Calories: 220
Fat: 9g
Saturated fat: 1.5g
Carbohydrates: 11g

Sugar: 3g
Sodium: 380mg
Fibre: 3g
Protein: 26g
Cholesterol: 65mg

22.　**Chilled Avocado & Zucchini Soup**

Prep Time: 5 minutes/ Cook Time: 5 minutes/ Total Time10 minutes/ Servings 6

Ingredients

- 2 leeks cleaned and thinly sliced
- 1 tablespoon olive oil
- 2 medium zucchini chopped
- 1 medium cucumber chopped
- 1/2 cup fresh cilantro
- 1/4 cup scallions chopped
- 1/2 teaspoon ground cumin
- Salt & pepper to taste
- 3/4 cup coconut milk
- 1 - 1 1/2 cups water
- 1 ripe avocado

Directions

1. In a small pan, heat the oil. Sauté the leeks for 3 to 5 minutes, before they are softened.

2. Add the leeks, cucumber, zucchini, cilantro, scallions, and spices to a blender, and blend until smooth. 1 cup water + 1/2 cup coconut milk using a high-powered blender, blend until the mixture is fully smooth.

3. Remove the lid and blend again until smooth, adding the avocado and remaining liquid.

4. If you want a thinner broth, add 1/4 cup of liquid at a time, mixing well after each addition, until you achieve your desired consistency. Season to taste and change seasonings if necessary.

5. Serve immediately if the soup has reached the target temperature. If not, chill until cold in the refrigerator.

6. To eat, ladle the soup into bowls and top with sliced zucchini, a drizzle of olive oil, and freshly cracked pepper, if desired.

Nutritional Values:

Serving: 2cups | Calories: 167kcal | Carbohydrates: 11g | Protein: 2g | Fat: 13g | Saturated
Fat: 6g | Sodium: 19mg | Potassium: 534mg | Fiber: 3g | Sugar: 3g | Vitamin A: 840IU | Vitamin
C: 21.6mg | Calcium: 47mg | Iron: 2.3mg

23. Roast pork with couscous & ginger yogurt

Preparation and cooking time Prep: 10 mins Cook: 40 mins Easy Serves 6

Ingredients
- 2 pork fillets, each about 500g/1lb 2oz, trimmed of any fat
- 2 tsp olive oil
- 3 tsp ground cumin
- 1 tsp ground cinnamon
- 4 tsp grated ginger
- 250g couscous
- 100g sultanas
- Zest and juice 1 lemon
- Small bunch mint, chopped
- 200g fat-free natural yogurt

Directions

1. Preheat oven to 190 degrees Fahrenheit/170 degrees Fahrenheit fan/gas 3. 5. In a non-stick frying pan, brown the pork for 4-5 minutes over high heat, rotating twice.

2. Rub the pork all over with a mixture of oil, 2 tsp cumin, cinnamon, 2 tsp ginger, and seasoning.

3. Roast for 30-35 minutes, or until the juices run clear when a skewer is inserted into the thickest part of the meat.

4. Season the couscous with the remaining cumin, sultanas, lemon zest, and juice, then pour 400ml boiling water over it. Stir well, cover, and set aside for 5 minutes before adding the mint.

5. Toss the yogurt with the remaining ginger and a pinch of salt and pepper. Serve the pork thickly sliced with the couscous and ginger yogurt.

Healthy Nutritional Value: per serving
Kcal 284
Fat 6g
Saturates 1g
Carbs 37g
Sugars 15g
Fibre 0g
Protein 23g
Low in salt 0.21g

24. Chicken curry recipe from Diabetic

Prep: 10 Minutes - Cook: 360 Minutes - Serves 4

Ingredients
- 1 large brown onion, roughly chopped
- 3 Tbsp. mild curry paste or gluten-free curry paste
- 400g can no added salt chopped tomatoes
- 2 tsp Messel Salt-Reduced Vegetable Stock Powder
- 1 tbsp. finely chopped ginger
- 1 yellow capsicum
- 4 chicken legs, skin removed
- 1 bunch coriander, leaves picked and chopped
- 2 x 250g packets microwave brown rice, to serve

Directions

1. In a slow cooker, combine the onion, curry paste, tomatoes, stock powder, ginger, and capsicum.

2. One-third of a can of water should be added. Stir all together thoroughly. Place the chicken on top of the other ingredients and force it down until it is fully submerged. Place the lid on top.

3. Cook for 6 hours on low heat, or until chicken and vegetables are very tender.

4. Just before serving, toss in the coriander leaves on top of the rice.

NUTRITIONAL VALUES:

PER SERVE 1740kJ, protein 26g, total fat 11g (sat. fat 2g), carbs 50g, and fibre 8g, sodium 636mg

25. **Low-fat rosaries**

Preparation and cooking time Prep: 10 mins Cook: 1 hr Easy Serves 2

Ingredients
- 800g roasting potatoes, quartered
- 1 garlic clove, sliced
- 200ml vegetable stock (from a cube is fine)
- 2 tbsp. olive oil

Directions
1. Preheat the oven to 200°C/180°C fan/gas 6. 6. In a roasting pan, put the potatoes and garlic. Brush the tops of the potatoes with half of the olive oil after pouring over the stock.

2. Cook for 50 minutes after seasoning with salt and pepper.

3. Cook for another 10-15 minutes, until the stock is consumed and the potatoes are browned and cooked through, brushing with the remaining oil.

Nutritional Values: per serving
Kcal 201
Fat 6g
Saturates 1g
Carbs 35g
Sugars 1g
Fibre 3g
Protein 5g
Low in salt 0.2g

26. **Baked garlic salmon with freekeh**

1:10 mints Prep Time/ 0:50 mins Cook Time/ 4 Servings

INGREDIENTS

- 1 teaspoon ground cumin
- 4 garlic cloves, crushed
- 2 tablespoons extra virgin olive oil, plus extra to serve
- 4 x 150g skinless salmon fillets
- 1 brown onion, thickly sliced
- 1 teaspoon mixed spice
- 2 teaspoons ground coriander
- 1 teaspoon ground cardamom
- 2 cups free keh, rinsed
- 1/4 cup no-added-salt
- Tomato paste 400g can crushed tomatoes
- 4 baby cos lettuce leaves, shredded
- 1/3 cup low-fat Greek yoghurt Lemon wedges, to serve

Directions

1. In a mixing bowl, combine cumin, 1/2 garlic, and 1 tablespoon oil. Season with salt and pepper. Toss in the salmon. Coat on the other hand. If time allows, refrigerate for 1 hour.

2. Preheat the oven to 200 degrees Celsius/180 degrees Celsius fan-forced.

3. In a 6cm-deep, 20cm x 30cm flameproof roasting pan, heat the remaining oil over medium heat. Toss in the onion.

4. Cook for 5 minutes, stirring occasionally, or until softened. Mix in the remaining garlic, blended spice, ground coriander, and cardamom.

5. Cook for 1 minute, or until fragrant, stirring occasionally. Freekeh is a delicious addition. 1 minute of stirring Tomato paste should be added last.

6. To mix everything, whisk it together. 1 litre water, plus crushed tomatoes Protect yourself. Bring the liquid to a low boil, then reduce to a low heat. Preheat oven to 350 degrees.

7. Preheat oven to 350°F and bake for 25 minutes, or until freekeh is nearly finished.

8. Through the freekeh mixture, nestle the salmon. Bake for another 10 to 15 minutes, or until freekeh is tender and salmon is just finished.

9. About the salmon, fold lettuce into the freekeh mixture. Season with pepper and a dollop of yoghurt on top of the salmon. Extra oil and lemon wedges are served on the side.

Nutritional Value:
3128 kJ ENERGY
26.6g FAT TOTAL
5.7g SATURATED FAT
20.6g FIBRE
47.9g PROTEIN
98mg CHOLESTEROL
278mg SODIUM
78.1g CARBS (TOTAL)

27.   **Spinach & Bacon Egg Cups**

Prep Time: 5 minutes Cook Time: 15 – 18 minutes Total Time: 20 – 23 minutes Yield: 24 mini egg cups 1x

Ingredients
- 6 eggs
- 3 tablespoons milk
- ¾ cup finely chopped spinach
- 1 cup shredded Cheddar cheese
- 4 strips bacon, cooked and chopped
- ¼ teaspoon black pepper

Directions
1. Preheat the oven to 350 degrees Fahrenheit and grease a 24-cup mini muffin pan.

2. Whisk the eggs and milk in a big mixing bowl. Chop the spinach and combine it with the shredded Cheddar cheese, chopped bacon, and black pepper.

3. To mix everything, whisk it together. Fill muffin cups halfway with the egg mixture.

4. Cook for 15 to 18 minutes in a preheated oven.

5. Enable mini quiches to cool in the pan before carefully removing them with a small knife or spatula once they are finished.

Nutritional Value:
Serving Size: 4 mini egg cups
Calories: 188
Sugar: 0.7g
Sodium: 329.7mg
Fat: 13.9g
Saturated Fat: 6.1g
Carbohydrates: 1.6g
Fibre: 0.1g
Protein: 13.6g
Cholesterol: 212.8mg

28.   Winter vegetable pie

Prep time: 15 mins Cook time: 45 mins Easy Serves 4

Ingredients
- 2 tbsp. olive oil
- 2 onions, sliced
- 1 tbsp. flour
- 300g (about 2 large) carrot, cut into small batons
- ½ cauliflower, broken into small florets
- 4 garlic cloves, finely sliced
- 1 rosemary sprig, leaves finely chopped
- 400g can chopped tomato
- 200g frozen pea
- 900g potato, cut into chunks
- Up to 200ml/7fl oz. milk

Directions

1. 1 tablespoon oil, heated over medium heat in a flameproof dish Cook for 10 minutes, or until the onions are softened, then add the flour and cook for 2 minutes more.

2. Cook, stirring occasionally, for 5 minutes, until the carrots, cauliflower, garlic, and rosemary have softened.

3. Pour a can of water and tomatoes into the vegetables. Cover and cook for 10 minutes, then remove the lid and continue cooking for another 10-15 minutes, or until the sauce has thickened and the vegetables are cooked.

4. Season with salt and pepper, then add the peas and cook for an additional 1 minute.

5. Meanwhile, cook the potatoes until they are tender, about 10-15 minutes. After draining, return the potatoes to the saucepan and mash them.

6. Stir in enough milk to achieve a soft consistency, then season with the rest of the olive oil.

7. The grill should be heated up. Fill a pie dish halfway with the hot vegetable mixture, top with the mash, and gently fork over the surface. Place under the grill for a few minutes, until golden brown on top.

Nutritional Value: per serving

Kcal 388
Fat 8g
Saturates 2g
Carbs 62g

Sugars 18g
Fibre 11g
Protein 15g
Low in salt 0.3g

29. **Creamy broccoli and spinach pasta**

0:15 mins Prep time/ 0:20 mins Cook time/ 4 Servings

INGREDIENTS

- 375g dried high fibre fettuccine
- 400g broccoli, cut into small florets
- 1 tablespoon pepitas
- 1 tablespoon sunflower seeds
- 3 teaspoons extra virgin olive oil
- 1 brown onion, finely chopped
- 3 garlic cloves, crushed
- 2 teaspoons chopped fresh thyme leaves
- 1 tablespoon plain flour
- 2 eggs
- 375ml can evaporated milk
- 1/4 cup finely grated parmesan
- 100g baby spinach
- 1 teaspoon lemon zest
- 80g mixed salad leaves
- 1 tablespoon balsamic vinegar

Directions

1. Cook the pasta according to the package instructions in a saucepan of boiling water, adding the broccoli for the last 3 minutes of cooking. Float. Put the pan back in the oven.

2. In a large frying pan over medium heat, toast the pepitas and seeds. Cook for 5 minutes, stirring occasionally, until golden brown. Fill a cup with the mixture.

3. Fill the pan halfway with oil. Combine the onion and the garlic. Cook for 10 minutes or until crispy, stirring occasionally.

4. Garlic and thyme should be added at this stage. Cook for 1 minute, stirring constantly, or until fragrant. Toss in the flour and whisk to combine.

5. In a mixing bowl, combine the eggs, evaporated milk, and parmesan cheese. Season with salt and pepper.

6. Toss the pasta in the pan with the egg mixture and spinach. Toss for 1 minute over low heat, or until the pasta is coated in a smooth, thickened sauce. Seeds and lemon zest are sprinkled on top.

7. Season with salt and pepper. Vinegar-dress the salad leaves. Salad should be served alongside pasta.

Nutritional Value:

2561 kJ ENERGY
14.5g FAT TOTAL
3.9g SATURATED FAT
13g FIBRE

32.4g PROTEIN
105mg CHOLESTEROL
267mg SODIUM
80.3g CARBS (TOTAL)

30.   **Veggie rice pot**

Preparation and cooking time
Prep: 10 mins
Cook: 25 mins
Serves 4

Ingredients

- 1 tbsp. sunflower or groundnut oil
- 2 peppers (one red, one yellow), deseeded and thickly sliced
- 250g pack shiitake or chestnut mushrooms (I used shiitake)
- 250g long grain rice (not the easy-cook type)
- 2 garlic cloves, finely chopped
- 1 heaped tsp five-spice powder
- 3 tbsp. dry sherry (optional but worth it)
- 140g frozen petits pois
- 1 tsp sesame oil
- 2 eggs, beaten
- Bunch spring onions, sliced diagonally
- 1 tbsp. light soy sauce, or more

Directions

1. Make a pot of water to boil. In a big, deep frying pan, heat the oil until it shimmers, then add the peppers and mushrooms. Fry for 3 minutes over high heat, or until golden brown.

2. Reduce the heat to low and add the rice, garlic, and five-spice powder to the pan. Splash in the sherry, if using, and top up with 350ml hot water after 2 minutes of sizzling.

3. Cover and cook for 15-20 minutes, stirring occasionally, until all of the liquid has evaporated and the rice is tender. Last few minutes, add the peas.

4. Add a drop of sesame oil to a new frying pan, then the eggs. To make a thin omelette, swirl the pan around. Turn out onto a cutting board, roll up, and shred thinly once it has set.

5. Place the egg and spring onions on top of the rice, fluff with a fork, and season with soy sauce and sesame oil before serving.

Nutritional Value: per serving

Kcal 377
Fat 9g
Saturates 2g
Carbs 67g
Sugars 9g
Fibre 4g
Protein 12g
Low in salt 1.14g

31. Diabetes-Friendly Chocolate Chia Smoothie Recipe

Total Time: 10 min Prep Time: 5 min Cook Time: 5 min Servings: 2 (1 1/2 cups each)

Ingredients
- ½ cup unsweetened almond milk
- 2 tablespoons chia seeds
- ½ teaspoon cinnamon
- 1 ½ medium frozen bananas, cut into chunks
- 1 ½ cups unsweetened almond milk
- 2 tablespoons cocoa powder
- 2 tablespoons peanut butter powder

Directions

1. Whisk together almond milk, chia seeds, and cinnamon in a medium mixing cup. Allow the chia seeds to swell and absorb the liquid for at least 10 minutes.

2. In a blender, combine the banana, almond milk, chocolate powder, and peanut butter powder. Puree until it is well blended.

3. In two glasses, divide the chia pudding. Serve immediately with the smoothie on top.

Nutritional Values (per serving)

198 calories
8g fat
31g carbs
6g protein
Total Fat 8g
Saturated Fat 1g
Cholesterol 0mg
Sodium 178mg
Total Carbohydrate 31g
Dietary Fibre 9g
Total Sugars 11g Includes 0g Added Sugars
Protein 6g
Vitamin D 2mcg
Calcium 588mg
Iron 3mg
Potassium 623mg

32. **Chicken Bella**

Prep Time 15 minutes Cook Time 35 minutes Total Time 50 minutes Servings 4 People

Ingredients

- 6 oz. grape tomatoes or cherry tomatoes
- 1 lb chicken thighs or breast, boneless and skinless
- 2 oz. Pancetta or diced bacon
- 2 cloves garlic fresh, minced
- 1 cup chicken broth
- 8 oz. cream cheese
- 4 cups spinach fresh
- 1/4 cup mozzarella cheese shredded

Directions:

1. Tomatoes should be cut in half. Roast the tomatoes for 25 minutes at 400 degrees on a baking sheet lined with parchment paper.

2. Preheat a cast iron or stainless steel skillet while the tomatoes are roasting. If using a whole chicken breast, pound it to an even thickness. Remove any excess fat from the chicken. If needed, slice.

3. In a large skillet, combine the chicken and pancetta. Brown until the meat is almost finished.

4. Sauté for another 5 minutes with the garlic. Place the chicken on a tray.

5. Pour chicken broth into the skillet, scraping up any browned bits from the bottom with a spatula.

6. Cream cheese should be melted over medium heat. When the sauce has reached a smooth consistency, stir in the spinach. Stir until the spinach has wilted.

7. Stir in the chicken and roasted tomatoes gently. Sprinkle with mozzarella until the dish has returned to room temperature.

8. Serve with an Italian-dressed green salad.

Nutritional Value: Amount per Serving
Calories 408
Calories from Fat 270 %
Fat 30g
Saturated Fat 16g
Polyunsaturated Fat 0.1g
Monounsaturated Fat 0.02g
Cholesterol 108mg
Sodium 763mg
Potassium 266mg
Carbohydrates 6g
Fibre 1g
Sugar 3g
Protein 25g
Vitamin A 3800IU
Vitamin C 19mg
Calcium 150mg
Iron 2mg

33. **Super healthy salmon burgers**

Prep time: 20 mins Cook time: 10 mins Serves 4

Ingredients

- 4 boneless, skinless salmon fillets, about 550g/1lb 4oz in total, cut into chunks
- 2 tbsp. Thai red curry paste
- Thumb-size piece fresh root ginger, grated
- 1 tsp soy sauce
- 1 bunch coriander, half chopped, half leaves picked
- 1 tsp vegetable oil
- Lemon wedges, to serve
- For the salad
- 2 carrots
- Half large or 1 small cucumber
- 2 tbsp. white wine vinegar
- 1 tsp golden caster sugar

Directions

1. Combine the salmon, paste, ginger, soy, and chopped coriander in a food processor. Pulse until the mixture is approximately minced. Remove the mixture from the bowl and divide it into four burgers.

2. In a non-stick frying pan, heat the oil and fry the burgers for 4-5 minutes on each side, turning halfway through, until crisp and cooked through.

3. Peel carrot and cucumber strips into a tub with a swivel peeler in the meantime.

4. Toss with the vinegar and sugar until the sugar has dissolved, then add the coriander leaves and toss again.

5. Using 4 plates, divide the salad. Combine the burgers and rice in a serving dish.

Nutritional Values:

Calories 630
Calories from Fat 320 %
Total Fat 29g
Saturated Fat 28g
Polyunsaturated Fat 3g
Monounsaturated Fat 16g
Cholesterol 133mg
Sodium 181mg
Potassium 504mg

34.   **Low Carb Gourmet Diabetic Pizza**

Prep Time 10 minutes Cook Time 16 minutes Total Time 26 minutes Servings 8

Ingredients

- 3/4 cup super fine almond flour
- 2 cups mozzarella cheese finely shredded
- 2 tablespoons cream cheese
- 1/4 to 1/2 teaspoon sea salt (1/4 is enough unless you really love salt)

Directions

1. Preheat the oven to 175 degrees Fahrenheit (350 degrees Fahrenheit).

2. Pre-bake the low-carb pizza crust and arrange all of the vegetables on a plate to be used as toppings.

3. Cover the pizza crust with tomato paste and spread it out uniformly.

4. The ingredients should come first, followed by the cheese.

5. Remove the pizza from the oven after 12 minutes and allow to cool slightly before slicing into 8 pieces with a pizza cutter.

Nutritional Values:

Facts Low Carb Gourmet Diabetic Pizza Amount per Serving
Calories 650
Calories from Fat 351 %
Total Fat 39g
Saturated Fat 18g
Polyunsaturated Fat 2g
Monounsaturated Fat 16g
Cholesterol 133mg
Sodium 1991mg
Potassium 504mg
Total Carbohydrates 19g
Dietary Fibre 6g
Sugars 7g
Protein 34g
Vitamin A50% Vitamin C135% Calcium35% Iron11%2

35. **Diabetic Strawberry Cheesecake**

Serves/makes: 10 Prep time: 1 hour Cook time: 1 hour

Ingredients

- 2 cups graham cracker crumbs
- 1/3 cup reduced-calorie margarine, melted non-stick cooking spray
- 1 envelope unflavoured gelatin
- 1 cup skim milk
- 2 1/2 packages (8 ounce size) Neufchatel cheese
- 1 tablespoon lemon juice
- 2 teaspoons vanilla extract
- 3/4 cup Equal spoonful sugar substitute
- 3 cups medium-size fresh strawberries, halved
- 2 tablespoons Equal spoonful sugar substitute
- 1/4 cup low-sugar strawberry spread
- fresh mint sprigs (optional)

Directions

1. In a medium mixing cup, whisk together graham cracker crumbs and margarine.

2. Cooking spray a 9-inch spring form pan and press the mixture into the bottom and 1 inch up the sides. Bake for 8 minutes at 350 degrees F. Allow to cool on a wire rack once removed from the oven.

3. In a small saucepan, dissolve gelatine in milk for 1 minute. Cook, stirring constantly, for 2 minutes, or until the gelatine has dissolved. Allow to cool slightly before serving.

4. Using an electric mixer, beat the cheese until it is smooth. Gradually add the lemon juice and vanilla extract, beating well after each addition.

5. Gradually beat in the gelatine mixture, scraping down the sides as required, until smooth. Mix in 3/4 cup sugar substitute until just combined.

6. Pour the mixture into the crust that has been prepared. Chill for at least 3 hours, or until mounted.

7. In a medium saucepan, combine strawberries, 2 tablespoons sugar substitute, and strawberry spread. Cook, stirring continuously, over medium-low heat until the spread melts and the strawberries are evenly covered.

8. Place the strawberry mixture on top of the chilled cheesecake. If needed, garnish with mint sprigs.

Nutritional Values:
Calories 322
Calories from Fat 41.2 %
Total Fat 15g
Saturated Fat 8g
Polyunsaturated Fat 2g
Monounsaturated Fat 5g
Cholesterol 36mg
Sodium 348mg
Potassium 172mg
Total Carbohydrates 39g
Dietary Fibre 1g
Calcium 71g
Protein 8g
Vitamin A 818
Vitamin C 22
Iron 1

36. **Make-ahead mushroom soufflés**

Prep: 30 mins Cook: 15 mins Serves 8

Ingredients

- 140g small button mushroom, sliced
- 50g butter, plus extra for greasing
- 25g plain flour
- 325ml milk
- 85g gruyere, finely grated, plus a little extra
- 3 large eggs, separated
- 6 tsp crème fraiche
- Snipped chive, to serve

Directions

1. Remove the mushrooms from the heat after 3 minutes and set aside a healthy spoonful of the butter.

2. To make a thick sauce, add the flour to the rest, then blend in the milk and return to the heat, stirring constantly. Stir in the cheese, season with salt and pepper, and set aside to cool.

3. Preheat the oven to 200°C/fan 180°C/gas mark 6 6. Butter and line the bases of 8 x 150ml soufflé dishes with baking paper.

4. After whisking the egg whites until rigid, carefully fold them into the soufflé mixture. Cover the soufflé dishes halfway with cold water and bake for 15 minutes, or until golden.

5. Allow to cool before continuing (they will sink, but they are meant to). The soufflés can be made up to this point two days ahead of time. Chill, covered.

6. Turn the soufflés out of their bowls, peel off the lining paper, and place them on a baking sheet lined with small squares of baking paper when ready to serve. 1 tsp crème fraiche and a sprinkling of cheese on top of each soufflé, followed by the reserved mushrooms.

7. Bake for 10-15 minutes at 190°C/fan 170°C/gas 5 until slightly risen and warmed through. Serve with a sprinkling of chives.

Nutritional values
per Serving
Calories 650
Calories from Fat 351 %
Total Fat 39g
Saturated Fat 18g
Polyunsaturated Fat 2g
Monounsaturated Fat 16g
Cholesterol 133mg
Sodium 1991mg
Potassium 504mg
Total Carbohydrates 19g
Dietary Fibre 6g
Sugars 7g
Protein 34g
Vitamin A50%   Vitamin C135%   Calcium35%
Iron11%2

37. **Beef with Noodles**

Prep time: 15 mins Cook time: 20 mins Easy Serves 4

Ingredients

- 1 (3-ounce) package ramen noodles, seasoning packet discarded
- 1 pound 90% lean ground beef
- 1 green bell pepper, chopped
- 1/2 cup onion, chopped
- 1 can (14.5-ounce) diced tomatoes with roasted garlic
- 1 teaspoon Italian seasoning
- 1 teaspoon garlic powder
- 1/4 teaspoon salt
- 1/4 teaspoon black pepper

Directions

1. Noodles should be cooked according to package instructions, then rinsed and drained.

2. Brown ground beef in a medium non-stick skillet over medium-high heat. Remove the beef and set aside to drain.

3. Cook bell pepper and onions in same skillet over medium heat for 5 to 6 minutes, or until tender, stirring occasionally.

4. Combine the tomatoes, beef, Italian seasoning, garlic powder, salt, and pepper in a large mixing bowl.

5. Cook, stirring periodically, for 5 to 7 minutes, or until thoroughly heated.

   Cook for 1 to 2 minutes after adding the noodles. Serve the guests.

Nutritional Value-Servings Per Recipe*

Calories330
Calories from Fat 134
Total Fat 15g
Saturated Fat 6.4g
Trans Fat 0.7g
Protein 27g
Cholesterol 74mg
Sodium 317mg
Total Carbohydrates 22g
Dietary Fibre 3.1g
Sugars 4.8g

38. Peanut Butter and Cranberry Cookie Bites {Gluten-Free and Sugar-Free}

Prep Time 20 mins Total Time 1 hr 30 mins Servings: 30 Calories: 133

Ingredients

- 4 tablespoons butter , softened
- 1 cup Natural Peanut Butter
- 1 cup Swerve Powdered Sugar
- 1 1/2 cups Gluten-Free crisp rice cereal
- 1 cup unsweetened dried cranberries
- 1/2 cup chopped pecans
- 1 cup unsweetened flaked coconut
- 1 cup unsweetened all natural cocoa powder

Directions

1. 1 to 2 minutes in a large mixing bowl, cream together the butter, peanut butter, and powdered sugar until smooth and fluffy.

2. Combine the cereal, cranberries, and pecans in a mixing bowl and stir until all is well combined.

3. Make 1-inch bite-sized balls out of the mixture.

4. Coconut OR cocoa powder may be used to roll the balls.
   1 hour in the fridge

5. Until serving, set aside for a few minutes on the table.

Nutritional Value- Amount Per Serving

Calories 133
Calories from Fat 81 %
Fat 9g
Saturated Fat 3g
Cholesterol 4mg
Sodium 54mg
Potassium 123mg
Carbohydrates 12g
Fibre 2g
Sugar 7g
Protein 3g
Vitamin A 45IU
Vitamin C 0.1mg
Calcium 10mg
Iron 0.7mg

39.   **Beef Stroganoff**

Prep time 15 min Cook time 15 min Servings 5

Ingredients

- white (button) mushrooms (sliced) 1 1/2 cup
- onion(s) (minced) 1/2 cup
- all-purpose flour1 tbsp
- dry white wine   1/2 cup
- Dijon mustard 1 tsp
- fat free, low sodium beef broth 1 (14.5-oz) can
- fat-free sour cream 1/2 cup
- salt(optional)   1/4 tsp
- black pepper   1/4 tsp

Directions

1. Cook the noodles as directed on the box, except without the salt.

2. Over high heat, pour oil into a big sauté pan. Cook for about 3 minutes with the meat.

3. Taking the meat out of the pan Sauté for 5 minutes, or until the mushrooms and onion are starting to brown.

4. Cook for 1 minute after adding the flour. To deglaze the pan, pour in the wine and cook for 2 minutes. Get the beef broth and Dijon mustard to a boil. Reduce heat to low and cook for 5 minutes.

5. Return the beef to the broth, along with any juices, and cook for another 3 minutes. Simmer for 30 seconds with sour cream, salt (optional), and pepper.

6. Serve with whole-grain egg noodles as a side dish.

Nutritional Values- Amount per serving
Calories 275
Total Fat 7g

Saturated Fat 2.5g

Cholesterol 50mg

Sodium 250mg

Total Carbohydrate 29g

Dietary Fibre 4g

Total Sugars 3g

Protein 23g

Potassium 270mg

40. Caramelised carrots & onions

Prep:15 mins Cook:40 mins Serves 8

Ingredients

- 500g carrot , peeled and cut into long chunks
- 50g butter
- 1 tbsp. olive oil
- 8 red onions , peeled and quartered with root intact
- 3 sprigs thyme
- 1 tbsp. soft brown sugar
- 3 tbsp. red wine
- 1 tbsp. good-quality balsamic vinegar

Directions

1. Carrots should be blanched for 3 minutes in a pan of boiling salted water, then drained and patted dry.

2. Melt the butter and oil in a large skillet, then cook the carrots, onions, and thyme for 30 minutes over low heat, until golden.

3. Stir in the sugar and red wine, then allow to boil for a few minutes to remove the alcohol.

4. Cook for another 5 minutes after adding the vinegar, until the mixture is syrupy.

Nutritional Values

Calories 143
Calories from Fat 81 %
Fat 10g
Saturated Fat 3g
Cholesterol 4mg
Sodium 54mg
Potassium 133mg
Carbohydrates 12g
Fibre 2g
Sugar 6g
Protein 3g
Vitamin A 45IU
Vitamin C 0.1mg
Calcium 9mg

CONCLUSION

Unmanaged diabetes can build your danger of creating coronary illness. Diabetic patients are likewise in danger for visual deficiency, removal and kidney disappointment. Eating a sound eating routine is a major piece of the difficult exercise. By eating better, being all the more truly dynamic, and getting more fit, you can decrease your manifestations.

Finding a way ways to forestall or control diabetes doesn't mean living in hardship; it implies eating a delectable, adjusted eating routine that will likewise support your energy and improve your mind-set. This Diabetic cookbooks is extraordinarily planned remembering the conditions and body taste of somebody who is simply starting to follow diabetes supper plan.

In case you're searching for new plans to give a shot in the kitchen that are both solid and advantage your body and heart, at that point this is the cookbook for you. You don't need to surrender your #1 food varieties, you just need to extend your taste-bud skylines.

With the Ultimate Diabetic Cookbook for Beginners, extraordinary tasting dinners are never forbidden for individuals with diabetes.

This Diabetes Cookbook for Beginner's gives you all you require to make solid and diabetic-accommodating dinners. In this changed and refreshed release, you'll find that it is so natural to oversee diabetes through diet. With huge loads of new plans—large numbers of them veggie lover—and the most recent data on diabetes testing, observing, and support, this book will help direct you down a way to a better you.

CPSIA information can be obtained
at www.ICGtesting.com
Printed in the USA
BVHW010839060521
606416BV00016B/1339